ACCLAIM FOR *RAISING A SOUL SURFER*

Bethany Hamilton's story of a shark attack while surfing in Hawaii is nothing short of inspiring. The family "story behind the story" may be even more compelling. I loved reading about the Hamilton's life before, during and after the shark attack and how they turned a tragedy into a triumph.

Jim Burns, PhD
President, HomeWord
Author of *10 Building Blocks for a Solid Family* and *Faith Conversations for Families*

If you are a mother, you *must* read this book. Cheri reminds us that our children really belong to God. It is He who lets them breathe, He who knows how many hairs are on their heads, and He who is with them always . . . even when they are in the mouth of a shark.

Shelene Bryan
Founder of Skip1.org , Producer of *Like Dandelion Dust*

Raising a Soul Surfer is an amazing story of how God shows us, even through adversity, that there is triumph. There is hope to those who seek Him, and His love endures forever! As parents, we all have hopes and dreams for our children, yet as big as our plans are for them, they are so much smaller than God's! Through what could have been a devastating tragedy, the Hamilton family has shown that all things do work together for good to those that love Him (see Romans 8:28).

Barbara Cameron
Author of *A Full House of Growing Pains*

This engaging autobiography chronicles the story of an unusual family of surfers that resulted in the phenomenon of Bethany Hamilton. Anyone interested in Bethany's story, surfing or Hawaii in general will enjoy this lighthearted but truthful account of the lives of Tom and Cheri Hamilton, a couple of serious surfers who fell in love in Kauai, lived in a van, and raised their kids surfing from the time they were tadpoles. The drive and dedication the Hamiltons bring to their faith and surfing are showcased in this inspiring story in readable prose that will bring both chuckles and tears.

Toby Neal, LCSW
Therapist, Parent and Author

Spending time with Cheri Hamilton and the whole Hamilton clan during script development, pre-production, filming and beyond gave me a unique perspective on the family. Seeing their love for God and the love of God pouring out of them kept us focused on the true reason for producing the film *Soul Surfer*. Having the opportunity to have Cheri capture even more of the story in *Raising a Soul Surfer* helps fill in all the blanks that are left unfilled by a two-hour movie.

Rich Peluso
Vice President, AFFIRM Films/Sony Pictures Entertainment

I have been truly honored to know Bethany Hamilton, riding with her and sharing platforms where we witness people's hearts being deeply moved by her inspirational story and her faith in God. As a child going and growing through difficulties of having no limbs since birth, I understand the importance of a mother's role in one's life through storms that seem too big at times. Cheri Hamilton's testimony will touch and challenge anyone's perspective of life. Furthermore, her love for Bethany, her family and, above all, God will ignite a flame of faith and encouragement to all who read it.

Nick Vujicic
Founder, Life Without Limbs

RAISING A SOUL SURFER

ONE FAMILY'S EPIC TALE

RAISING A

soul surfer

CHERI HAMILTON
& Rick Bundschuh

Regal

From Gospel Light
Ventura, California, U.S.A.

Published by Regal
From Gospel Light
Ventura, California, U.S.A.
www.regalbooks.com
Printed in the U.S.A.

Cover photograph of Bethany by Noah Hamilton of Noah Hamilton Photography
(www.noahhamiltonphoto.com). Cover photograph of the Hamilton family by Mike
Coots of Mike Coots Photography (www.mikecoots.com).

All photographs © the Hamilton family archive and Noah Hamilton Photography,
except photo #9 (Hamilton family photo) © Steve Gnazzo of Kilohana Photography and
photo #20 (Timmy bodyboarding) © Shea Sevilla. Used with permssion.

Library of Congress Cataloging-in-Publication Data
Hamilton, Cheri.
Raising a soul surfer : one family's epic tale / Cheri Hamilton with Rick Bundschuh.
p. cm.
ISBN 978-0-8307-5969-9 (hard cover)
1. Hamilton, Bethany—Family.
2. Surfing—Wounds and injuries—Hawaii—Kauai—Biography.
3. Shark attacks—Hawaii—Kauai—Biography.
4. Amputees—Rehabilitation—Biography.
5. Christian biography—United States. I. Bundschuh, Rick, 1951- II. Title.
III. Title: One family's epic tale.
GV838.H36H37 2011
797.32092—dc22
[B]
2011007024

Rights for publishing this book outside the U.S.A. or in non-English languages are
administered by Gospel Light Worldwide, an international not-for-profit ministry.
For additional information, please visit www.glww.org, email info@glww.org, or write to
Gospel Light Worldwide, 1957 Eastman Avenue, Ventura, CA 93003, U.S.A.

To order copies of this book and other Regal products in bulk quantities,
please contact us at 1-800-446-7735.

contents

Foreword

"Don't look down," Bethany called out to me as we were surfing a reef break named "Freddy's" on the North Shore of Oahu. I kept eyeing the shadows and coral heads beneath the surface of the crystal-blue water, secretly convinced I had seen a shark. Bethany, in her chill, all-knowing manner, knew exactly what was in my mind and encouraged me to set aside my fears.

If you are that worried about sharks, don't surf. Fear can ruin a good time, and anticipating the unknown is futile. Ever since a shark attacked Bethany, she focuses on what she can control instead of what she can't see. In fact, "Don't Look Down" seems to be an unspoken motto for the entire Hamilton family. This expression is not a suggestion that they ignore their fears; rather, it is a statement of courage that motivates them to embrace life's challenges. Instead of worrying about what *might* happen, the Hamiltons trust in the Lord and don't blink an eye to transitory disturbances. They continue to look up toward the Lord, hoping and praying for good instead of mulling over their fears.

This unique family lives a beautifully rough island life, "following their bliss" and not fretting over what is around the next turn. Rather than analyzing and contemplating their next move, they taste life and experience it. This attitude represents an island mentality of living life to the fullest and simply enjoying the gifts God provides: the ocean, family and friends.

The Hamiltons and the island on which they live (Kauai) are all about community. But it's a kind of community that cannot be replicated. The ocean spiritually bonds people on Kauai. The desire and love for the ocean is in the heart of every Hamilton and seems to carry them from day to day, giving physically satisfying meaning to their lives.

During the past year, I've had time to get to know each member, and at this point they feel like extended family. I have found that although each of the Hamiltons has a love for the ocean, the similarities stop there. Tom (Dad) reminds me of a soft-spoken giant. He anchors the family, but he has the most kindhearted voice you'll ever hear. When I was staying at the Hamilton house during this past winter break, I went with Tom on their little boat to watch Bethany surf some big waves. I've never seen Tom grin so wide. He literally became so entranced by the enormous sets rolling in and the barrel-rides being caught that the boat almost capsized.

If one person could be the entire "coconut wireless," it would be Cheri Hamilton. Cheri never stops praying. When we were shooting a particularly dangerous shark-attack sequence one day, the crew and cast experienced sharp reefs, unruly waves, rising tides and a difficult setup. But in the midst of crewmembers running around and pandemonium setting in, Cheri gathered a few people on the set and prayed for safety. When tensions were high on set and a million different activities consumed every second, it was nice to know that someone was praying for God to watch over every move.

Noah, the oldest son, is the classic firstborn. He is always two steps ahead of the family, and usually most of the people around him as well. He dealt with just about every issue that came up on set, and because of his proactive nature, he, along with his wife, Becky, helped to make the film more accurate. *Soul Surfer* had a relatively low budget, and the production company didn't have finances for an on-set still photographer. So Noah, a professional photographer himself, offered his services. Becky, who has a multitude of high-level skills, also documented the action with their video camera. Now we have images of the cast and crew hard at work—a recorded behind-the-scenes documentary. Noah continually thinks of how to solve problems himself instead of relying on others to do the job. By now he feels like an older brother, and with all of his ingenuity and kindness, he will make a wonderful father to his soon-to-be-born baby!

Tim Hamilton, the middle child, has the disposition of a turtle. In Hawaii, that is a compliment! He is a natural waterman and is most content there. The first time I met Timmy was in the ocean. I had my first surf lesson with Bethany's surf coach, Russell Lewis, and Tim was out in the water playing "lifeguard" for me. Of course, Tim didn't have to look out for me—the film producers could have hired someone—but he took some prime bodyboard time to help me out. Tim lends a quiet hand whenever the need arises . . . never needing to be asked. Even though he says the least in the family, you have to keep your ears wide open around him. Tim is the person most worth listening to for his witty under-the-breath humor, which always makes me chuckle.

And now, Bethany . . . It is difficult to find words to explain my love and admiration for my friend and personal hero. She totally charges![1] I still do not understand how she pops up on such a little short board with one arm. I take for granted her tenacity and trust in God, because that's just the way she is. You cannot begin to compare her to anyone else on this planet. Bethany's godly behavior and playful determination have continually had a positive influence on my life and the lives of those around her.

I remember one particularly windy day when I wanted to surf. Bethany was available, so she took me out surfing. As soon as we arrived at the beach, I regretted my decision. The waves looked more intimidating than anything I had previously surfed before, not to mention it was close to sunset (of course, sharks eat at all hours of the day, so time should be irrelevant for me). Bethany eventually convinced me that I had "definitely ridden bigger waves," so I paddled out.

I was terrified. To me the waves seemed immense and life threatening, while to Bethany they probably seemed tame and barely large enough to have fun on. At one point, I endured a particularly gnarly wipeout (for me at least), but I'll forever be proud of the small scar the fin of my board carved on my leg. After my wipeout, I caught the longest and most enjoyable right of my surf career to date.[2]

After the ride was over, I couldn't wipe the smile off my face. And I have Bethany to thank—she pushed me and taught me not to "look down." Because she believed in me, I achieved a wave I never thought possible. Her presence ignites a vigor for life that is unique to anyone I have ever met.

Bethany, Timmy, Noah, Cheri and Tom, I want to thank you for welcoming me into your lives. You have shared with me your love for the ocean, so I want to share with you one of my favorite quotes that captures our beloved sea: "Unchangeable save to thy wild waves' play . . . roll on, thou deep and dark blue Ocean—roll."[3]

AnnaSophia Robb

Notes
1. "Charges": having no fear and going for big waves.
2. "Right": A wave breaking toward the right from the vantage point of the surfer riding the wave. From the beach it would be a wave breaking toward the left.
3. Lord Byron, "Apostrophe to the Ocean," *Childe Harold's Pilgrimage*.

Introduction

Greater love has no one than this,
that he lay down his life for his friends.

JOHN 15:13

Tom, my husband, and my daughter, Bethany, had gone
to Puerto Rico for a surf competition. Sitting at the computer, I
did a search for weather conditions. That region tends to get big
storms. I became concerned when I found hurricane Shary brewing, which is my name but with a different spelling. The weather
report also said that another hurricane, called Tomas, my husband's name, followed back to back and had stormed over Hamilton, an island town in Bermuda.

I was amazed at the irony of the names, because it described
in weather terms what life has been like for our family. At this
time, November 2010, our nephew had just died on the East coast,
and here on Kauai, everyone was in shock over the death of four-time world champion surfer Andy Irons, who had lived close by.

All of these unusual signs also acted as a confirmation to
put down on paper my reflections of the storm-surging changes
that have come upon my life and that of my family, as well as
the Island of Kauai.

My mother said that I didn't walk at seven months, I ran! Activity and energy have been a part of me from the start. I should have been a pro athlete, but at the time there were few options for women.

When I went surfing for the first time, my life was never the same. I soon committed my whole life and existence to catching the next wave. For the next 15 years, I lived to surf. I focused my everyday life on finding waves and only working jobs that allowed me to have time to surf.

When I met Jesus, I personally experienced His divine providence in a way that I could not walk away from, which guaranteed that I would never deny His existence. After I had invited Jesus into my heart, I knew that I had found the truth and, at last, that my deepest desire for love was fulfilled and complete in Him. His love filled a void in my heart that I had longed for all of my life.

At the beginning, I was a young surfer girl, living my dreams, who encountered God in an unlikely place through unlikely disciples. I was a surf gypsy, with a surf gypsy husband, enjoying life in a tropical paradise. But I became a mother who had to wrestle with fear and uncertainty when the news came that her daughter had been attacked by a shark. I never expected our children to be life-changers. We had raised our daughter to surf, not to be in the media spotlight. Yet she embraced this challenge to honor God and be His witness to the world.

Our story is about a violently shattered dream that was replaced with a bigger one. But most of all, our life story has been, and continues to be, about trusting God in spite of circumstances, pressures and unexpected events.

I've always wanted to be involved in some kind of Christian ministry, but every door closed for me; so I focused on raising my children for Him—teaching them His Word, His ways and His unconditional love. Unbelievably, it turned out to be the very ministry God was calling me to all along.

My story tells about a journey to find hope, truth and purpose. It encompasses the perspective of my husband, a sensitive yet strong father who struggled to make sense of a tragedy, and who had to learn to trust God all over again. It reveals my struggles to find love, hope and acceptance. It includes the perspective of my sons, Bethany's brothers, whose lives have been irrevocably changed by the sudden and unforeseen reverberations stemming from the choice our family made to allow Bethany's story to be told.

Most of all, this story is a glimpse into God's perspective as it has been revealed to us. Only in retrospect have we been able to see how far back His amazing providence has reached into our lives. His hand has always been active, and not just since the events of that fateful Halloween morning in 2003. From the beginning, God prepared our lives in so many ways for "such a time as this," just as He did for Queen Esther (Esther 4:14, *NIV*).

My hope is that by reading our story you will be encouraged to pursue God regardless of the cost. He doesn't take away or allow you to go through pain to hurt you, but to heal and transform and draw you to Himself. God's plan is not to leave us as He found us, but to fill our lives with His purpose and His hope for an amazing future filled with His love!

I cannot get enough of God's Word. The more I learn, the more I want to learn. His Word is so deep, fascinating and layered with insight and guidance that it is new to me every morning. God's Word is a book that can be read for a lifetime without ever plumbing its depths. It is filled with the story of His love for each and every person that He has ever created. His Word tells us about hope and a future plan He has for everyone (see Jeremiah 29:11).

One of my favorite Scriptures, in which I put my hope, is, "No eye has seen, no ear has heard, and no mind has imagined what God has prepared for those who love him" (1 Cor. 2:9, *NLT*). I like to encourage others with the words of Psalm 37:4: "Take delight in the LORD, and he will give you your heart's desires" (*NLT*).

When I turned to Christ, I found a love in Him so pure, so perfect and so real that I wanted with all of my heart for everyone to know His amazing love too. My true purpose in life is that I want to share Jesus with the whole world.

I write these words 30 years after I accepted His grace into my life. Through all of the pain and the joy, I still revel in the wonder of His love. I invite you to see the extraordinary things God has done in our *Ohana* and become a part of it as you say yes to God and His perfect love for you!

Cheri Hamilton
Kauai, Hawaii

Hollywood Comes
to Paradise

*Now to him who is able to do immeasurably
more than all we ask or imagine.*
EPHESIANS 3:20, *NIV*

"Surreal!" Tom said.

That is the word my husband used a lot to describe the swirl of events that have swept up our family during the last seven years. This was the word he used on a recent spring morning to describe what took place on the pristine, exclusive grounds of Oahu's Turtle Bay Resort.

Turtle Bay is much like the five-star resort on Kauai that Tom has worked at as a waiter for so many years; but now he was waiting in a golf cart for his partner. As usual, he had one eye on the crystal-blue waves peeling along the point.

He smiled and made room for his partner. He had never met this man until today, but he couldn't shake the feeling that he already knew him.

As the bagmen loaded up the cart, they meekly approached Tom's golfing partner. "Excuse me, sir," one of them said, gesturing toward two golfers standing off to the side, resplendent in their Ping shirts, Callaway saddle shoes and Adidas gloves.

"Those gentlemen over there are wondering if they could join you two this morning."

Tom's partner was gracious, but shook his head. "Tell those guys, no offense, but I just want to spend some time with my friend Tom."

Then, actor Dennis Quaid, who had been hired to play the role of Tom in the movie *Soul Surfer* that was about to start filming, slid into the driver's seat of the golf cart and spun the ignition switch. Off they went.

Tom tried to remember the movies he'd seen this iconic American actor in over the years: *The Rookie, Dragonheart, Far From Heaven, The Big Easy, Vantage Point, Flight of the Phoenix, Yours, Mine and Ours*...

My husband thought he wouldn't be able to get over the fact that Dennis Quaid wanted to spend the morning hanging out with him, but as the day progressed, a connection grew between them that went beyond a Hollywood actor researching a role. It shifted toward a friendship.

Dennis started out with a little notepad, which Tom figured he was going to use to record notes as he studied him. But after a few minutes, he put it down and never touched it again. As they made the rounds on the beautiful, tropical golf course, Dennis peppered Tom with questions about our family and about raising our kids in Hawaii. He talked freely about his career and about those whose film work he admired.

He also discussed his own family. As someone who had faced family tragedy himself, Dennis talked about the well-reported time when hospital staff mistakenly gave his 10-day-old twins a dosage of heparin 1,000 times the common amount for infants, almost killing them.

Tom listened quietly as the persona of an actor and Hollywood personality melted away and Dennis simply became a loving father who had nearly lost his precious children.

Dennis explained, between the sand traps and putting greens, how he had ended up playing the role of my husband for the movie. "I was playing with my kids on the living room floor one morning when your daughter, Bethany, came on a television show. I remembered that a shark had attacked her. I turned up the volume. When I heard what she had to say, I realized what an amazing young girl she was. Her story touched and inspired me more deeply than you can know. When the show's host said there was a movie in the works about Bethany, I thought, *Now that's something I'd like to be a part of.*

Tom said that Dennis got quiet, even misty-eyed, as he recounted it. Tom could sense the power of the moment and remained silent.

When Dennis spoke again, he turned to Tom and grinned that famous, bright grin and said, "Wouldn't you know it, a few weeks later my agent called and told me that the producers were wondering if I would like to be part of a movie about an impressive girl named Bethany Hamilton from the Hawaiian island of Kauai. I jumped at the chance!"

Tom said then, and again when he got home, "It was a God thing."

In our wildest dreams, neither Tom nor I could have imagined the events that have unfolded in our lives, nor could we have imagined the path our journey would take as a family. I don't mean just the well-known shark attack on an early Halloween morning in 2003. I mean all of the many paths and events that brought us through that near-tragic point and to the present where Tom was playing golf with a talented actor who would be using his talents to tell our story.

I knew beyond a shadow of a doubt that if I had been in charge of writing the script of our lives, I would have written it much differently than God did. But God's script is certainly more incredible! I would describe it as like standing behind a tapestry of God's creation. From my vantage point, I can't see the pattern or the purpose. Life is often stormy, conflicting and seemingly senseless, like the aftermath of a hurricane. Then, every once in a while, God lets me see the front side of the tapestry.

I know that even my husband's playing golf with Dennis Quaid, and the way Dennis seemed to have been summoned to play the part of Tom, has been God-orchestrated. For example, Tom had no idea as he shared his faith in Christ that the actor had been raised in a Christian home and Dennis had made strong statements about his own Christian faith.[1]

It was *all* a God thing; divine providence!

We had waited a long time, seven years, for the day of filming *Soul Surfer* to arrive. But, finally, everything was in place, and in February 2010, our family moved to a house in front of a popular North Shore surf spot called V-land, on Oahu, for the production of the movie.

We were in the epicenter of the surfing world, in the part of Hawaii known as the Seven Mile Miracle, named for the string of world-famous surf breaks found there, such as Pipeline, Sunset Beach and Waimea Bay. The North Shore is where the majority of big wave contests are held and where pros go to train. Others migrate to these prime waves just for the pure passion and love of the sport of surfing. Many others with iron-willed grit challenge the bigger waves the size of multi-story houses grinding into shallow, razor-sharp reefs. If you've ever seen footage of a big-wave surf competition, 9 times out of 10, you're looking at the Seven Mile Miracle.

Moving into our new home for the next couple of months included shipping Hana, our dog, over from our home on Kauai, so that the family would be complete. We could cook our own food and eat together as a family versus staying in a hotel room. We could also have family meetings about the production work in progress. We could even spin up the road on Sunday to attend church with our friends at North Shore Fellowship after an early morning surf session.

In case you were wondering what kind of Hollywood perks we got . . . it didn't include maid service. That was my *kuleana*, or responsibility, although everyone pitched in! Sometimes while Tom was out playing golf with the likes of Dennis Quaid, I played "mother hen" at home.

The making of *Soul Surfer* was not my first time on a set, but I'll admit I'd hardly paid any attention to the many movies in production on Kauai, because the surf always took precedence on my radar.

Our home island, Kauai, and in particular, the North Shore where we live, has been featured in dozens of major movies—such as *South Pacific, Jurassic Park, Raiders of the Lost Ark, Outbreak*—and most recently, *Pirates of the Caribbean: On Stranger Tides*. When the scenic taro fields of Hanalei in *Uncommon Valor* were turned into rice paddies for the Viet Nam effect, we could just pretend Kauai was under attack on our way to go surfing!

I remember the time, just before hurricane Iniki hit, when I was driving past some giant green gates in the middle of a cane field that read "Jurassic Park" on the gates, and wondering what in the world a "Jurassic Park" was. I'd never even heard of it. But now, the production of *Soul Surfer* had at last become a reality. We, as a family, were all in the thick of it. Tom, Bethany and I watched and learned the involved process of making a movie. Through this very rare opportunity of seeing a production team working together to create the story about our family, we came to the set each day. Noah and Becky were hired as co-producers to help fine-tune many important details, some small and others very big. They were involved intimately in and made a difference in casting, locations and music.

In a movie theater, the action moves along quickly; but in order to create those fast-paced, fluid scenes, there is a massive amount of work and time to get it just right. Making a movie is meticulously detailed work. The daily expenses of making a movie required long workdays to take advantage of the good weather. Every tiny nuance is elaborated on, which sometimes takes weeks even before the actual filming begins! We filmed for two months on Oahu, a few days on Kauai, and a week in Tahiti. Every detail in the script, every rewrite—and every rewrite of a rewrite—every contract detail took up most of everyone's time and energy. Once the official filming began, it was exciting to watch; and on occasion, we were able to contribute a tip here and there.

Sean McNamara, the director, who is so talented and has such a congenial personality, did not need too many tips. His creative talent made the whole production a positive, family-friendly movie.

It was fascinating to watch the scenes being shot, but it was also sometimes difficult from a mom's and dad's perspective. One time, we came to the set late in the morning when they were filming a scene at the Hamilton house, just when the family was giving thanks at the meal. Ross, who played our son Noah, didn't know what to do when they all took hands to give thanks. AnnaSophia, who played Bethany, saw his discomfort and placed his hand on her shoulder. I had just looked into the monitor to watch, and I broke! I started crying because the scene was so realistic.

Tim, Bethany's brother, was hired to be a part of the camera crew. He had an asset envied by all—huge calves! When you are filming a surf movie, it means beaches with soft sand. No one wants to carry heavy equipment for long distances across soft sand. But wait! Look at those calves! They can go anywhere! Do anything we ask! Go, Timmy, go! We need you!

God had pre-prepared Tim for years to do a fine job for his sister's movie. He had already made two body boarding DVDs and short films full of humor, creativity, and storytelling. Tim's prowess in the water is legendary. He is as strong as an ox in and out of the water. He already had a reputation for super endurance, boldness and fearlessness in all his endeavors. He went on to be an assistant on the *Hawaii 5-0* TV drama. He has a huge amount of talent and I am thankful as a mother that God has chosen to use him.

We were very happy with the cast of exceptional actors. We as a family were concerned because they needed to be convincing as real surfers in the water. But no need to worry!

Dennis Quaid was caught up by the surfing passion. That meant that not only did Dennis look good in the water on a surfboard, but he also didn't need to act! At one point, Dennis kidded that my husband had ruined him as a golfer by introducing him to surfing. His heart was fully immersed and caught up by riding waves. For the rest of his time on Oahu, he surfed as much as possible even until the day he had to ride his last wave at Makaha and head for the airport while still wet!

Helen Hunt, whose job it was to play my "surf mom" role, was already an avid surfer and brought her own favorite surfboard to use in the movie. On our few days off, we would all go surf longboards. She really has great grace and poise as she drops down the face of a wave. The hottest surfer was Helen's surf coach, "Turtle," who outshined us all! He costarred in the retro classic surf movie *North Shore*. One of my favorite lines in the movie is when she said no to night surfing but then changed her mind. I often did the same thing.

The most significant role in the movie went to AnnaSophia Robb, who plays my daughter, Bethany. Not only did Anna-Sophia have to look like a natural surfer, but she also had to surf with one arm behind her back!

When Bethany and I saw *The Bridge to Terabithia* starring AnnaSophia, we both agreed that she was the perfect actress to play the part. One area we felt was important to accurately portray was how Bethany adapted so amazingly after what should have been a debilitating loss. The shark took Bethany's left arm all the way up to the shoulder. Most of us don't realize just how difficult it is to do the simple little chores of life without a limb. Buttoning a shirt, tying shoes, making lunch—all the everyday things that most people do without thinking about it.

AnnaSophia had highly skilled teachers for the surfing scenes. Her Oahu coach was big wave surfer Noah Johnson. Noah was the surfing stunt double riding the amazing barrel at Pipeline in the movie *Blue Crush*. He is a well-known big wave surfer on the North Shore of Oahu and won the Quicksilver Eddie Aikau big wave competition at Waimea Bay back in January 1, 1999.[2] On Kauai, AnnaSophia worked with Bethany's own world-famous surf coach Russell Lewis, who sets up his lessons out of Hanalei Surf Company. (He is a former Australian Junior Champion.)

AnnaSophia was a quick study for surfing, partly because she'd been involved with dance, gymnastics and swimming in school. She is a natural athlete like her father and has the gracious charm of her mother. We gave her an A+ as a beginner!

Jack Nicholson's daughter played Alana with such a natural finesse. Loraine is a charming young actress in front of the camera. She did a great job barfing on the beach just like the real Alana did after the shark attack! Loraine made us cry, but she also made us laugh while she skillfully played Alana with an uncanny likeness. Noah Johnson coached Loraine Nicholson for the more serious role that she had to play.

Sonya (Balmores) Chung is married to Noah's friend Kanoah, who is an avid and talented surfer on Kauai. In real life, Sonya, an excellent surfer, competed against Alana and Bethany in their younger years. Noah was walking by some of the producers in the office and overheard them discussing who could play the part of Malina Birch. They were considering an actress from outside the U.S. when Noah suggested Sonya Chung, a surfer and local Hawaii actress. God has His perfect timing!

Ross Thomas and Chris Brochu, who play our sons, Noah and Tim, were both already natural watermen. They matched our sons' characters perfectly. It was fun watching everyone surf Makaha; and afterward, Chris often entertained us with his guitar and singing.

Kevin Sorbo was matchless in his role! He naturally fit the part of Holt, just like a real hero, and was the perfect surf dad to Alana, Holt's daughter, played by Loraine Nicholson. For his surf lessons, Kevin chose to focus on what he needed to know to look cool and confident on the beach and in the water. He needed to look like an experienced surfer and got tips on detailed aspects of surfing, such as holding his surfboard in a natural manner against a strong wind; how to wax a surfboard like you have been doing it for 35 years; and (this is critical) how to walk across the reef during the rescue scene with very rough waves breaking on the rocks along with an incoming tide! This was one of the toughest scenes to shoot in the whole movie.

Bethany suggested that Jeremy Sumpter, who starred in the 2003 movie *Peter Pan*, play the role of Byron, Holt's son, and the producers agreed. Because of the movie time constraints, his role was limited. The most physically challenging scene in the movie is when Kevin and Jeremy rescue Bethany right after she loses her arm. The camera crew, and even the director, had to live in their wetsuits for days as pounding surf bombarded them. The medic was kept busy with reef cuts and coral implants! Kevin handled it all like a champ.

Arlene Newman-Van Asperen, who plays Sydney, Alana's mother and Holt's wife, is a Hawaii girl from the North Shore of Oahu. Naturally, Arlene fit right into the surf scenes for the movie. She has studied acting for years and won Mrs. Hawaii in 2005. Arlene was my regular prayer partner during the making of *Soul Surfer*. She is gracefully skilled and gifted at Hawaiian dancing. She grew up involved in church, as her father is a minister and her mother a strong prayer warrior. We called her mom a few times to request prayer when we were feeling overwhelmed! Arlene's part was small, but she got to hang out with Kevin Sorbo!

Sarah Hill, Bethany's youth pastor, was hired as a makeup artist. She had met Jesus as her Lord and Savior in Southern California. While surfing a California beach break, she took a bad wipeout and broke her neck and back. God miraculously healed her. Prayer was a strong point in her spiritual life, which is how she received divine direction to move to Hawaii. No one believed her, but she chose to trust God's guidance. She made the move over to Kauai and settled in as a youth leader at North Shore Community Church where we attend. Sarah built friendships with the girls through surfing and Bible study; then the shark attack occurred.

Carrie Underwood landed this key role as youth leader in the film. I believe she fit her role perfectly and had a powerful impact on the outcome of the scene where she spoke the words of Jeremiah 29:11. After going back and forth on whether to keep the verse in the script, the battle ended when Carrie stated that it was a part of the real story and we all should honor the family's wishes.

As believers on the north shore of Kauai, we have fellowshipped and gathered in the name of Jesus at many different locations. Our church has never had our own "home," where you put down solid material roots, housing such tools as a Christian library with loads of great books, DVDs, kids' videos, a prayer chapel, a fine-tuned nursery or an actual building to meet midweek for worship and Bible studies and other gatherings.

Presently we meet under a yellow and green tent with a beautiful shade tree for our prayer chapel.

When the film director Sean McNamara came over to scout out locations for certain scenes, he attended church with us under the tent. But this wasn't where we attend church; it was at Becky's father's church, where he is the worship leader/assistant pastor. Raise your hand if you meet under a tent to worship God! And raise your hand if your son has married a beautiful girl who also meets for worship under another tent! We were on a time crunch and this service fit into the tight schedule. After all, what is the difference between one tent and another? (Visitors must think that here on Kauai we all meet in tents for church services!)

The day we showed up at the beach park for shooting the church tent scene, which I thought was going to be filmed on Kauai but wasn't, I was taken by total surprise. The scene was gloriously beautiful. A white tent was set up on the grass next to the sparkling blue water at a beach park in Kahuku. Tears filled my eyes as I looked on the scene. A large standing wooden cross was set up outside and was included in a scene. And it was so special to watch Timmy work with the camera crew. He has a very amiable personality, and the crew enjoyed working with him. Tom and I, along with some of our friends and some friends and family of other key people, were in the church scene as extras. Imagine that! We got paid to go to church!

Tom and I sat behind Dennis Quaid and Helen Hunt. Then we all sang the special theme song God had given our family right after the shark attack, "Blessed Be Your Name," written by Matt and Beth Redman. We sang it over and over, for take after take after take, but I never got tired of it. We sang it with different angles and slight adjustments, and it was fun, fun, fun!

The funniest part of filming the scene related to our daughter-in-law, Becky, working her job as co-producer. Because Sean McNamara is himself a talented musician, he is great at managing the music scenes. Sean put Becky in charge of keeping us, the worshipers, on track as we sang. Becky's hand stuck out from behind a curtain and went up and down in time with the proper beat as the cameras rolled on us. All we could see was this hand leading worship. It was hilarious! Later, because we spent most of the day filming the tent church scene, the cameras focused on the worship team, which included Becky leading worship along with Carrie Underwood, a friend of Noah's and a girl from San Diego.

The Sunday after Bethany left the hospital after the attack, we all attended church together. For the last song, the worship team played "Blessed Be Your Name," and God totally spoke to me through that song. Some of the words say, "He [God] gives and takes away! Blessed be His name!" We rejoiced together in the truth that no matter what happens in our lives, we are in His hands and He orchestrates our experiences for His divine purposes. This song gave me so much peace. We knew that our heavenly Father was reaching out to us to let us know that He watches over us.

With God's impeccable timing, this song was played in every church service we attended as we traveled during the next year—Australia, New Jersey, England, California, Haleiwa, and many other places. It was a confirmation that we were in His will. At the end of this season, during which I was going through a trial, I asked God to confirm an issue of my heart by playing "Blessed Be Your Name" at church—He did it! I was very surprised and felt very loved by Him.

When the boys were little, I noticed that they had opposite personalities. Timmy had singular focus while Noah had a myriad antennae all tuned in to anything and everything that was going on. Noah's ability to multitask came into play in countless ways in the making of *Soul Surfer*. His tenacious spirit helped him become part of the production team. Heaven provided Becky, our son Noah's wife! She had recently graduated from California State University Fullerton with a degree in filmmaking. Noah and Becky were hired as co-producers to help fine-tune many critical details, some small and others very big. For instance, Noah was a stickler about the clothes that would or would not be worn by surfers portrayed in the movie. They both were involved and made a difference in casting, locations and music. Noah made sure the surfing scenes were kept as authentic as possible.

Except for the few who already knew how to surf, the cast of *Soul Surfer* was schooled on just how difficult it is to balance on a chunk of slick-glassed foam while thousands of pounds of churning water propel you either toward rocks or reef or crashing shorebreak. I know that surfing looks easy; but trust me, compared to almost any other sport, the learning curve for advanced surfing is almost vertical.

You can fast-track your beginner surfing experience with lessons on safety, etiquette and the main surfing skills to minimize your mistakes and possible injuries. It may sound as if no one would want to go back after a challenging day of surf lessons, but the crew of *Soul Surfer* really got with it. Having the right equipment, the right weather and wind conditions, along with perfect beginner waves, one can quickly learn the basics and enjoy riding the warm waves here in Hawaii.

The most important aspect in the film was showcasing Bethany's real surfing abilities, which Noah promoted in Tahiti. Becky was on set every day, advising Sean, our director, about every detail with dialogue, surf lingo and the accuracy of Bethany's portrayal. Noah worked on the water unit team that spent hours filming the competitions. He helped head up and organize the Kauai unit for some of the most dramatic backdrops used in the film. Noah and Becky worked long hours assisting the art department, wardrobe, product placement and stock footage. As one of the set photographers, Noah documented the daily shoots with still photography while Becky videoed the same.

As the filming of *Soul Surfer* progressed, we focused on helping to bring out the real details of the story rather than fiction. There are too many facts in the whole story that are not believable! The entire family, especially Noah and Becky, took great pains to ensure that the film realistically portrayed the surf culture, island life and, of course, our Christian faith. Noah and Becky also rounded up any and all of our Oahu friends to work and be a part of the surf contests or church crowd.

We were especially pleased that Noah was able to get Mike Coots, his friend from surfing, who lived a few houses away from us when we were living in Kilauea, Kauai, involved in the film. Mike had lost his foot to a shark attack in 1998. This occurred while Mike was body boarding on the west side of Kauai with a group of friends who were all highly ranked competitors in the contest arena. He lost the lower part of his leg but survived by fighting the shark off with his bare hands. Like Bethany, Mike didn't let his loss keep him from enjoying the ocean. With the help of a specially designed prosthetic leg, he has learned to stand-up surf along with continuing his passion for body boarding.

Mike went on to get a photography degree at Brooks Institute in Santa Barbara, California. In the film, he plays the part of a photographer shooting Loraine Nicholson, who is playing Alana in the beach photo shoot scene in *Soul Surfer.*

Mike and Bethany's stories are similar: Each was given a choice whether to be defeated or to come back stronger. These days, Mike keeps busy as a professional surf and lifestyle photographer, as well as speaking in defense of sharks from destructive fishing habits such as "finning" (cutting off the fin for food consumption and medical uses, and discarding the rest of the fish, often alive).

Still young, adventurous and full of energy, Mike and another buddy, Miguel, towed the rotting carcass of a wild boar out into the ocean with a jet ski. Miguel waited, finger on the ignition, as Mike lowered a video camera strapped to a long paddle. It wasn't too long before a 16-foot tiger shark appeared and snatched the pig down in one gulp!

There is a lot of down time while scenes are being set up, but everyone seemed to make use of that time to catch up on endless cell phone calls. Sadly, this diminished the opportunity to get to know and interact with others on the set. Turning off all of those phones was critical during each scene take.

With the strong trade winds and saltwater, the hairdressers were at their wits' end. So you won't see your favorite hairdo in *Soul Surfer*! When you're surfing, you don't care how your hair looks. Actually you may care, but there isn't too much you can do about it while getting tossed and turned by the waves. It was an unending task keeping the actors looking like movie stars.

Just being able to have our friends and family involved with us on this amazing project gave us a deeper sense of connection to the incredible fact that a movie was being made about us . . . about how a terrifying event on an October morning didn't destroy us, but instead became a mighty outpouring of unprecedented blessing in our lives and in the lives of others.

A tsunami came to the Hawaiian Islands on February 27, 2010, during the movie production. An 8.8 magnitude earthquake had struck in faraway Chile. Immediately, seismologists warned that a possible 3- to 7-foot tidal wave would race from one end of the Pacific to the other.

Hawaii was right in its path.

Years ago, in the 1950s, our next-door neighbors told us they had lost their oceanfront house in a tsunami but survived by immediately climbing the hill behind their house when they noticed the receding waters in the bay. I realized that tsunamis are something to take seriously. So when the air raid sirens started blaring at 6:00 A.M. on February 27, Sean disrupted our filming schedule and had everyone seek safety. The Turtle Bay Resort had rooms that were three stories high where they recommended the guests, actors and producers retreat.

We stayed put as the phone book tsunami inundation map showed we were high enough on the hill to avoid the surge. We could look out of our window and watch as the neighbors packed up their barbecues, surfboards and jet skis.

We had packed up a car more than once for tsunami alerts in the past. They have all hit but were too small to be of real concern. I researched and knew nothing would endanger us, so we figured this would be an opportunity to catch a few un-crowded waves!

We loaded the car with surfboards and the camera after we saw the report that no tsunami was hitting other Pacific island locations in the path from Chile. The kids had a great surf ses-sion until the coast guard helicopter hovered and harassed them to leave the water. I have done intensive research on tsunamis and we have lived through so many false alarms that we were sure this one would have no impact. We have experienced so many really huge surf days that a three-foot surge among the regular waves is not going to keep us up on a hill.

Later, sitting on the beach, I realized that God was showing me a metaphor not only for the film we were making, but also for what has happened in our lives. The event that could have been a tsunami of destruction and fear has turned out to be a wave of blessing. God has always had a plan for us, and He only used the perceived tragedy to advance His plan and embrace the world with a tsunami of love. It was the fulfillment of Jeremiah 29:11 in our lives.

We were in the middle of God's plan and we saw how He was using our lives to draw people to faith in Him. I could see that God has always kept us in His care. He was preparing Tom and me before we even knew Him personally and intimately.

The event that rocked our family didn't send out destruc-tion; it sent out a wave of hope and love in the form of a story of triumph over adversity through our trust in God. The tsunami of God's impact in our lives has not run out of energy. In the telling of our story, people are still being swept off their feet by God's love.

Our journey to this place began long before that shark attacked Bethany. It began far away from the lush tropical beaches of Hawaii. It began with a New Jersey boy in thick square-framed glasses, and an athletic blonde California girl in San Diego.

Notes

1 Laura Sheahen, "'It's All God': Interview with Dennis Quaid," Beliefnet. http://www.beliefnet.com/Faiths/Christianity/2005/11/Its-All-God-Interview-With-Dennis-Quaid.aspx.
2. "Hilo Hawaii's Noah Johnson Wins the Quicksilver in Memory of Eddie Aikau," HoloHolo Hawai'i, January 1, 1999. http://holoholo.org/quikeddy/q990101.html.

Jersey Boy

*The L*ORD *will fulfill his purpose for me; your love, O L*ORD*, endures forever—do not abandon the work of your hands.*

PSALM 138:8, *NIV*

Tom was 13 years old when he discovered the joy of surfing.

Does New Jersey strike you as a likely place for a thriving surf culture? News spreads fast and even faster in the surfing world. In August 1888, the cover of a magazine called the *National Police Gazette*, a New Jersey publication, featured a female surfer riding on a wave. This piece of East Coast history is documented by Skipper Funderburg and is part of the Surfing Heritage Foundation collection.

Fast track to 1963, when the Beach Boys had a mega hit song with "Surfing USA." With the help of music, it seemed as if surf fever was catching on everywhere—including the barrier island resort town of Ocean City, New Jersey.

Tom's dad moved the family there from central New Jersey when Tom was a toddler. Tom's dad was a dentist, and I guess he figured he could fix teeth anywhere, so it might as well be close to the beach. So Tom, the youngest, and his two brothers, Mike and Bob, and sister Pat, found themselves in quaint and family friendly Ocean City, a small town of around 8,000 people that swelled in number every summer. When summer rolled around, Ocean City's famous boardwalks were crowded to bursting with a great view of friendly, rideable waves.

During that summer of 1963, the only thing that mattered to Tom and his best friend, Monk, were the waves peeling across the water off the jam-packed beach—waves that suddenly had a new meaning: Surfing!

For most Americans, surfing was just another novelty fad like the hula-hoop or 3D movies. Surfers were daredevils riding monstrous waves in Hawaii, or hanging 10 in bikini-clad California—both faraway places from Tom and Monk's everyday world.

With his strong swimming background, it was a natural course of events that Tom found something to pursue outside of the pool. Of all his siblings, he was the rowdy one, the restless one, the "Trickster," as his surf crew named him. His nickname came not because he was mischievous, although that was true as well, but because he could do some tricky things with a pool stick.

Tom got booted out of parochial school for pelting one of the sisters with an eraser. You can imagine that his good Irish Catholic parents might have thought they had their hands full with their fourth child, especially since they only meant to have three children.

Tom's parents were steadfast, and like many in their generation, they made sure everyone was off to Mass each Sunday. It was more than just what they did; it was part of who they were as a classic Irish Catholic family.

As much trouble as Tom caused the poor nuns, and for all his complaining about those boring church services, if you asked my husband about it now, Tom knew that the seeds of the gospel were planted in his heart because of the consistency and devotion his parents demonstrated in their faith.

Church wasn't the only activity that was important to them. The Hamiltons were an athletic family, and the ocean was a big part of their life. They were all strong swimmers, including Tom's mother. His parents actually met in a swimming pool on an ocean liner going to Ireland. Each was in college and already engaged to another but fell in love—hook, line and sinker—on the Atlantic Ocean. Tom's brother Mike received swim scholarships and became a teacher at Atlantic City High School. He also became the school's swim coach, and he was a lifeguard at the beach every summer until his retirement.

Like his brother, Tom also was a swimmer throughout high school, but it was surfing that truly grabbed his heart and soul. Right there at the end of Ocean City High School, across the crowded boardwalk, clean rideable waves came racing out of the Atlantic to curl along the sand bar next to the Music Pier. If you wanted to surf, you needed to have the right equipment to enjoy riding the waves.

With youthful determination, Tom's best friend, Monk, got his hands on a surfboard. The '60s era surfboards, or tankers, as they were nicknamed, were clunky, oversized boards and weighed almost as much as your typical 13-year-old. The board was too heavy to carry alone.

The waves kept enticing from the end of the boardwalk, but there was no way that Monk could haul the board down to the beach. It might as well have been across the country. So the two boys came up with a plan. They would share the board and carry it together to and from the beach.

All that summer the two of them could be seen lugging around that giant board, Tom clutching the nose and Monk the tail, as they made their way across town. They learned to surf in shifts, taking turns on the one board they had between them.

There was another serious hurdle Tom had to overcome in order to improve in his surfing. He was (and still is) very near-sighted—so much so that he wore thick black-rimmed glasses, not something you can wear in the saltwater and breaking waves. Without glasses, he was lost and disoriented in the water. Tom could not see the waves coming until they were right on top of him.

So Tom learned to rely on the feel of the water as it shifted and to anticipate the movement of other surfers around him. He knew that when everyone else suddenly paddled off toward the horizon, a set of waves was coming in. He learned to surf in an instinctively sensitive technique.

Years later, in Hawaii, Tom had his late takeoffs wired. He was known for surfing one particularly harrowing surf spot—a reef break where he'd drop into the waves with wild abandon, taking off at the last second. I said something about how crazy he was to take such late hairy drops, as if he lived for thrills. Usually, when surfers see a big set coming, everyone paddles hard to pick up speed to drop into a wave. If it is too late to drop in, you can have a very nasty wipeout, especially when the waves have some size. Tom confessed to me that his bravado came from his poor eyesight. He could never really see just how late his takeoff was, so he perfected his instincts and learned to drop into the biggest and gnarliest waves somewhat blindly. Amazingly, he made the drop most of the time.

Ocean City, New Jersey, in the summer of 1963, was the watershed for Tom. He and Monk immersed themselves in the small world of New Jersey surfing. By Labor Day, the boardwalk shut down after a summer of activity. The stores, the many eateries, the amusement parks along the boardwalk, the miniature golf parks all closed down for the winter and the Shoe-bees (a slang term for the summer-time visitors, who brought their lunch in a shoe box) crawled back home in the end of summer traffic. By the time school opened, Tom and Monk were fairly proficient and completely hooked on surfing.

With the hint of coming winter in the air, the boys surfed after school and on weekends, knowing their time was running out before the winter snows fell. They went out as soon as dawn made the waves visible and until the setting sun had faded into darkness. Neither of the boys had a wetsuit, so when the weather started to turn, eventually it became just too cold to surf. Reluctantly, they put the surfboard into hibernation up in the garage rafters.

It must have felt like the longest winter ever before the new year thawed and the weather warmed enough to get back into the water. For his birthday, Tom's father bought him his first surfboard. He got it at the local hardware store, and in spite of the Hawaiian name and fancy logo, it was an authentic "pop out" board—a cheap mass-manufactured surfboard. Tom didn't care; it was his!

Tom's dad later admitted to him that he almost regretted ever buying him that board. "That's the moment I lost you," he would say. The sport of surfing, not family, school or church, became the driving force in Tom's life from that moment on.

That first summer went by in a flash of surf, surf and more surf. Both Tom and Monk quickly learned to check the buoys and scour the weather reports for swells generated by hurricanes and tropical storms moving up the Atlantic. But even without the bigger, faster waves generated by these storms, there were plenty of good fun waves to be had on the shifting sandbars along the coast. As the warm days drew to a close, the boys knew they had to find a way to surf all year round.

We're still talking about New Jersey here . . . in the winter. Tom tells our kids, who are spoiled by the year-round warmth of the tropics, wild stories about coming out of the ocean with icicles forming on his hair and eyebrows and having fingers so numb that he had to ask strangers to put the key in the car door lock.

Of course, our children can't relate to what he is saying at all.

Somehow, both Tom and Monk scrounged up enough money for wetsuits. These weren't the nice, flexible wetsuits we have in today's surf shops; back in the early sixties, those things were crude, clunky and expensive. They were made for diving, not surfing, and were beyond uncomfortable.

Tom and Monk had to grease their armpits with Vaseline to avoid getting a chafing rash from the rigid neoprene as they paddled. Then there was the whole buttoning, yanking, tugging on of the whole contraption, including a ridiculous-looking beaver tail that was supposed to keep icy water from rushing up into the jacket. And then top off the whole affair with booties, gloves and a hood that would barely let you turn your head. They had to work hard to enjoy the winter swells.

With the stores along the boardwalk shuttered until spring, and the amusement rides closed down, the sight of two young boys waddling through the snow in those seal suits, surfboards balanced on their heads, must have been a bizarre sight to the few year-round Ocean City residents. With stiff movements because of the wetsuits, and chilled to the bone, the boys would surf in the freezing water until they could no longer endure it.

But was it ever worth it! If the beaches and waves were crowded during the summer, the surfing population of Ocean City shrank dramatically in the winter. No more than a few dozen surfers were part of the hard-core crew that surfed year round in these adventurous conditions. By the time spring rolled around, these daring young surfers celebrated its return and their survival with a Polar Bear surf contest.

Like all young surfers, when the surf was flat, Tom spent idle hours hanging out at the local surf shop. Eventually, George, the owner, asked him if he wanted a job. Thinking of how he'd be able to afford his own custom-made surfboard to replace his beat-up old pop-out, Tom agreed. He was a fast learner, and soon George taught him the art of repairing surfboards.

With the summer crowds, it was inevitable that surfers would crash their boards into each other, into the pier or into some hardheaded tourist who swam out too far. Then there were all the guys who were a little too careless in tying their boards down on car roof racks. Step on the gas and—*whoop!*—board goes flying off. It didn't matter if you were part of the hard-core crew or a weekend warrior, eventually you'd ding up your board.

Soon, as business picked up, repairing surfboards became the only thing Tom did for the surf shop. Because he had been well trained, Tom could speed through the work of the day and still have lots of time to surf. And because he now had a job, he was finally able to purchase his own custom surfboard. Even to this day, when traveling with Bethany in the professional surfing circuit, it's not uncommon for Tom to turn their hotel room into a repair shop stacked with boards awaiting his attention.

When not surfing, Tom and his surf buddies spent hours poring over the surfing magazines that featured crisp blue waves towering over the iconic surfers of the day. Those waves didn't resemble anything off the New Jersey beaches, not even on those big days when violent storms in the Arctic Circle created perfect icy tubes to tempt surfers across the snowy sand for a quick barrel and an instant ice-cream headache.

No, the waves in those magazines were on distant shores: California, Hawaii, Mexico. Tom dreamed about paddling into waves like that. All he asked his parents for, over and over, was a surf trip across the country to California. For his graduation gift, in the summer of 1968, Tom got his wish. He was 18 years old, and it was his first time on an airplane; but that new thrill paled in comparison to the fact that he was finally going to surf in the Pacific Ocean.

Tom, my future husband, flew into California with visions of a surfing paradise, but his visions paled in comparison to the wonderful land of Southern California that greeted him.

The palm trees, the miles of coast, the endless waves, the girls . . . it was like he'd died and gone to heaven. Everywhere he turned there was a famous surf spot, and the waves themselves! They didn't look like this back where he came from.

Tom ended up in Hermosa Beach, California, in the South Bay area of the Los Angeles basin. For a few wonderful weeks he prowled up and down the Pacific Coast Highway hitting surf spot after surf spot, from sunup to sundown. Then, tanned, satiated, yet already dreaming of his next surf trip, Tom flew back home to New Jersey.

A surprise awaited him in the mailbox, one that would change his life forever.

A draft notice.

Ticket to 'Nam

*Trust in the Lord with all your heart and lean not
to your own understanding; in all your ways acknowledge
him, and he will make your paths straight.*

PROVERBS 3:5-6, *NIV*

When Lee Harvey Oswald pulled the trigger on that fateful day in Dallas, in November 1963, Vice President Lyndon B. Johnson inherited the Oval Office and a war. The conflict that became the Vietnam War had been building since World War II. By the time John F. Kennedy was assassinated, it was rapidly escalating.

For most Americans, the tension in Southeast Asia was a distant annoyance that took a backseat to what was happening in Cuba and the arms-and-space-race with Russia. But what seemed only to be a slow cooking "police action" began heating up under LBJ as more Americans were shipped overseas, and more were sent back in flag-draped boxes.

More than any other war or conflict since the U.S. Civil War, Vietnam divided America. The politics, the protests . . . the fabric of the nation that had been woven so tightly by the preceding generations was suddenly coming unraveled.

By 1968, the country was in turmoil over the policies that spawned the war, over the point of the war and its cost, and there was an ever-deepening mistrust in the government. It seemed like every person under 30 was busy squaring off in rowdy and, sometimes, violent confrontation against anyone seen as "The Establishment."

It was a time of counterculture and conflicting ideology. People questioned what it meant to be a patriot; they questioned America's purpose. I was in the sixth grade when, one day after school, I answered a knock at the door. There I saw two men in black, complete with government-issue sunglasses. The men identified themselves with their FBI badges and asked to see my father. He was home for the day after teaching American history, and the agents informed him that he was to not talk negatively to his students about America's involvement in Vietnam.

Tom has always told me that he was oblivious to any of this. His whole world was surfing—a world far removed from politics, protests, wars and all its horrors. Perhaps he was unusual for a young man of his generation, but Tom thought, talked and dreamed of nothing but surfing.

So it was with dread that he pulled the slim, official-looking letter out of his mailbox. The words "selective service" above a notification to present himself to the United States military induction center in Philadelphia for a physical suddenly brought that wider world rushing in upon him.

Tom's friends told him not to worry; the Army doctors would most likely reject him. Not only did he have bad eyes, flat feet and a hammertoe (which made wearing military boots and hiking for long periods of time unfeasible), but like other surfers of that era, he also had "surfer's knots" on his knees and feet. These were large, protruding calcium deposits that developed as a result of extended kneeling on a hard surface. (Even the apostle James was nicknamed "old camel knees" by the Early Church because he reputedly spent so much time on his knees in prayer!)

Before shortboards, surfers used to paddle on their knees, with their feet tucked up underneath them. Today's surfers lie prone because the small size of surfboards do not facilitate knee paddling. Back then, those knots were an insider's mark of dedication to surfing. And they were also usually a ticket out of military service.

Most Army doctors had never seen a surf knot, and so the first batch of surfers to show up for an induction physical were stamped 4-F—physically unfit for military service. Of course, most of the surfers appreciated the irony of being rejected, and certainly they weren't letting on that this mysterious affliction that marred an otherwise fit and athletic-looking man would shrink harmlessly away after a few months off the surfboard.

Bolstered by these assertions of a 4-F stamp, Tom waited for the date of his physical and drove the 70 miles to Philadelphia. The induction center was jammed with guys like him, all 18 to 20 years old. Tom filled out a few forms and was ushered into a room where he was given a multiple-page test that started with a basic problem such as drawing a line from the picture of a screwdriver to the object that matched it; nut, nail or screw.

Of course, whole rows of guys intentionally answered every question wrong, thus guaranteeing themselves a position in the infantry. Tom answered the questions honestly, trusting in his 4-F knees, feet and eyesight. After the test, Tom was conducted to a locker room where everything he had on besides his undies were stripped off and stashed away. Paperwork in hand, he was told to follow the white line to the physical evaluation station. Tom looked down at his knotty knees and gnarled feet and trudged along without complaining.

What he didn't know was how great the military's appetite for new troops had grown and that the acceptable physical standards were dropping rapidly. Tom passed the physical with flying colors and was told he had three months of freedom before he belonged wholly and irrevocably to the United States Armed Forces.

Right about then, Tom paid attention to the war his nation was wrestling with. As his time on the outside dwindled, he dreaded being stuck crawling neck-deep in jungle mud as a grunt—avoiding land mines, snipers, booby traps; lying in foxholes; catching malaria. You name it—he knew he didn't want any part of it.

Tom's swim coach turned out to be a commander in the Navy Reserves, and he graciously used his connections to help Tom get an enlistment into the Navy. This is an example of when "who you know" counts at a turning point in your life.

At the end of his three months, he reported to Lakehurst Naval Air Station in New Jersey, for boot camp, and boy did he get a rude awakening.

The life of a surfer has its own sort of regimentation, its own discipline and endurance. But the military regimentation, discipline and tests of endurance are a far cry from the self-imposed life of a dedicated surfer. Being yelled at by drill sergeants; called every name in the book and all the ones not in the book; being forced to march, stand, wake, eat, dig holes, fill holes, at any time, with no seeming rhyme or reason—all were a bit of an adjustment for Tom. He still laughs about being "leader of the pack" to do punitive pushups.

Boot camp spit him out, and soon after, Tom got his orders. Only four months after his California Dreamin' surf trip, Tom found himself heading back to California, to North Island Naval Station in San Diego, where he was assigned to the Navy destroyer *USS Hanson*.

Because he could type well, Tom ended up with the opportunity to work in and be in charge of the ship's post office—a particularly enviable job in the days before electronic media, because a letter or package from home was the only way that family and friends could communicate with their loved ones at sea. The postmaster was appreciated by the crew, so much so that Tom was often given little gifts by happy sailors out of the care packages he delivered—homemade cookies, dried fruit and then some.

While most of the time the ship's postman was treated like a good fellow by most of the crew, there was one petty officer who resented the fact that Tom, a wet-behind-the-ears kid, had pulled such light duty. He took every chance to harass Tom until one day it came to a head. The two men found themselves in a "smoker"—an officially sanctioned boxing match where enlisted men could settle their grievances by pure force.

The officer was bigger and more experienced than Tom, but Tom's father was a true fighting Irishman who'd won many bouts in his youth, including a national championship at age 12. He passed on a few of his fatherly fighting tips to his son, and after years of surfing, Tom was in better shape. He eventually knocked the other guy down and finished the fight. But that only made things worse. Ego bruised, the officer's grudge burned fiercer.

Tom decided that there was a better way to fight back, and since direct action hadn't worked, this time he'd try something non-confrontational but effective. Every time the mail came in for Tom to sort, he quietly hid anything destined for the petty officer in the ship's safe—which only he and the captain had access to.

Every mail call, the officer watched as everyone else got letters and packages from home while he got nothing. The officer couldn't understand it; his wife wrote him regularly, even numbering the letters.

Tom could see the suspicion and frustration building. The guy knew something was up, but he couldn't prove anything. Four mail calls later, Tom handed the officer a huge packet of numbered mail wrapped in rubber bands. Tom never gloated or threatened, but from that moment on the harassment ended.

For a while, Tom and the *USS Hanson* patrolled on standby along the California coast. The crew was kept busy with menial tasks of sanding, painting and scrubbing. While the Vietnam War raged on, and the nation fractured over it, it looked like they wouldn't be deployed. When the call came down, they had only three days' notice before getting underway for the Gulf of Tonkin and war.

But war was still distant in Tom's mind. He enjoyed being out on the open ocean and would often escape the sights, sounds and smells of seasick crewmen below deck by climbing the signalman's bridge to stand in the open air and watch waves bowl over the bow of the ship during storms.

Love of the ocean kept him up there even when it meant getting thoroughly soaked. And the deep, rolling Pacific, miles from shore, fed his soul. He would look out across the expanse of never-ending blue and think of perfect waves peeling along some hidden coast.

Tom had already figured out who the surfers were aboard the *Hanson* because of the surf magazines coming to them through the mail. One of them was a young body surfer named Rob, who hailed from Oahu. Rob was always talking about the brutal shore break at Makapu'u, or about how much better the waves were in Hawaii than anywhere else.

"You should surf some *real* waves!" he would kid Tom, "Not those itty-bitty-kiddie waves they have in California or the East Coast." Instead of being goaded to defend his home breaks, Tom recalled the pictures splashed across every other page in the surfing magazines, showing Hawaii as a surf Mecca, a tropical feast of nonstop perfect waves.

You can imagine how excited Tom was in knowing that the first port of call was Pearl Harbor. At last he'd made it to Hawaii, though arriving by Navy destroyer was not the way he'd imagined. Tom couldn't wait to get off the ship. It was only a short stop, but Tom and some of the others managed to surf Waikiki. It was Tom's first experience with the warm Hawaiian waves.

"And just think, if you moved to Hawaii you would never have to wear a wetsuit again!" Rob told him with a grin.

He had no idea just how appealing this was to Tom.

But the day drew to a close and they had to report back to the ship. In the morning, they sailed out of the peaceful fiftieth state and toward war.

There were a few other ports of call, and though Tom had never been out of the country, unlike a lot of the men on his ship, he was not particularly enchanted with the seedy rows of flesh dens, grimy bars and alleys full of con artists aggressively trying to hustle any sailor they could. In particular, he remembers Subic Bay in the Philippines as inciting both pity and revulsion for the desperation with which people hounded the sailors—offering everything, including themselves, for money or cigarettes or trinkets.

Not to mention that Tom recalls that sick bay was always full after the more infamous ports.

From Subic Bay, Tom's ship escorted the aircraft carrier *Kitty Hawk* to Vietnam, where they anchored a mile offshore, providing fire support for the marines and army onshore.

The blast of the huge guns spewing explosive shells deep into the jungle was exhilarating at first, but when Tom started to listen in on the accuracy reports, he was faced with war in a way that conflicted and disturbed him. Over the headset, he heard artillery spotters report that the shells had missed their mark and landed on a village of "friendlies." Tom sat in silence, trying not to imagine the innocent men, women and children snuffed out by his ship's guns. He tried to dismiss them as collateral damage, like the guy on the radio did, but it haunted him.

Still, he had an enviably safe job, miles offshore, far from the brutal field conditions and persistent violence and horrors of war. Sometimes he got to head into the nearby base via helicopter, on a "milk run," ferrying bags of mail to and from the ship. But overall, his war experience was cushy. The things that happened in the wet jungles couldn't touch him.

Tom's nonchalant sense of security came to an end during a standard milk run over a dense rain forest that was supposed to be enemy-free.

The Vietnam War had come for Tom.

To this day, Tom won't talk about it. So I let what happened remain in obscurity. Maybe someday he'll be ready to talk about it, or maybe not. I can respect that he doesn't want to ever revisit his experience.

But I do believe that the shock of "this can't be happening to me!" that Tom got that day in Vietnam was a kind of preparation, or maybe a dress rehearsal, for the similar dismantling of our own nest of casual security when we first heard that our daughter, Bethany, had been viciously mauled by the second most dangerous shark in the world.

Vietnam could be blamed on politicians and revolutionaries. In the case of Bethany, when Tom wrestled with the very real possibility of losing his daughter forever, there seemed to be only one person to blame . . . God.

CHAPTER

4

Destiny

My times are in your hands.

PSALM 31:15, *NIV*

My dad was born in Denver, Colorado, and he lived his life with a high level of activity and adventure. I can get dizzy watching the home movies my mother took in the early years of their marriage.

In high school, he was a super athlete and achieved a high level of skill in most sports. His abilities are showcased in back-to-back clips of skiing, gymnastics, tennis, high dive and swimming laps—including the breaststroke, butterfly and crawl. He is shown horseback riding, ice-skating, cross-country skiing, and more.

After high school, he joined the Marines and was recruited to play on their football team. His team won the annual United States Football Championship two years in a row at Quantico, Virginia, against the Army! After his military commitment, he was able to go to college on the G.I. bill, in Denver. He studied and worked hard to make it on his own, while barely surviving on peanut butter and crackers.

In his last year of college, my parents met on a double date, although they were not paired with each other. My mom was attracted right off and nabbed a date with him soon after, followed by marriage and the birth of my older sister, Debbie. After completing his four-year degree at Denver University, my dad landed his first teaching job in a nearby mountain town called Glenwood Springs. Dad and Mom packed up my one-year-old sister, Debbie, and Grandma Julia, and moved to their new home.

Glenwood Springs was not only my birthplace, but also the place where I first fell in love with water. In Glenwood, hot volcanic mineral springs bubble up to fill what was the largest swimming pool in the world back in 1953. This premier pool was the first training ground for two future surfer girls. The pool stays open all year round, even in the dead of winter when you can immerse your tired muscles and achy bones into these naturally hot, healing waters under glittering snowfall or a starry summer night.

My dad took his first position teaching history and coaching the wrestling team. This meant traveling on weekends to various high school competitions. Late one night, while my dad was away at a competition, my mom went into labor. Without a car, she left my sister asleep in the crib while she, accompanied by Grandma Julia, carefully walked over icy sidewalks in the falling snow to the small hospital clinic. It was 4:00 A.M. on Valentine's Day, 1953, when I came into the world, ready to fall in love with the water and begin training to live my ocean-bound life.

My parents were probably the most regular swimmers at the hot springs pool. We have photos of my sister and me jumping into the pool as babies. It must have been easy to become water babies where the land is covered with several feet of freezing snow and the pool water is warm and wonderful!

After two years in snowy Glenwood Springs, my dad took a new job in the dusty, dry desert of Arizona, at Yuma High School. We found a house in a family neighborhood with lots of desert critters. We missed the hot springs pool back in the mountains of Colorado, so my mom came to our rescue. She had our backyard paradise fenced in to keep out the rattlesnakes, and then she made a water park playground to cool us off. We turned brown from playing in our kiddie pool under the blazing Arizona sun.

My younger sister, Karin, soon arrived. When she got big enough, she was put in charge of squirting us with the hose. My mom kept busy washing diapers, which were completely dry by the time she hung the last one up. This was a big change from the frozen diapers hanging stiffly on the line in Glenwood Springs! My mother took great care of us. She sewed beautiful little dresses for Easter, enrolled us in ballet dance classes, curled our hair and made the best taquitos ever! My dad, though, was California dreaming. He worked extra after-school hours selling cars to save up vacation money to scout out San Diego.

During the summer break, our family would pack up our station wagon and go camping on just about every beach in California. We went everywhere along the ocean, which helped my dad confirm his decision to move to San Diego. He loved the beaches, the zoo, the beautiful harbor; and he set his course to eventually move to this wonderful beach-lined city. It wasn't long before his winning reputation as a wrestling coach at Yuma High caught the notice of a football coach at San Diego High. I once asked him about his two state championship victories in Yuma. He said the real secret to his success was the amazing talent of his team who were mostly Navaho indigenous people.

At last, our ocean-bound destiny became a reality. We packed up our Ford Fairlane station wagon and moved to San Diego.

You might get the impression that my parents liked to move around a lot. But the truth is, once they got to San Diego, California, that was it. Looking back, I can only thank God.

Like Tom, my family ended up living near the beach. But you can hardly get any farther removed from New Jersey beaches than sunny Southern California, where I grew up. Once I hit elementary school, I was firmly ensconced in the idyllic fifties-era childhood—Barbie dolls, roller skates (they had steel wheels back then), and Saturday movie matinees, complete with Giant Sweet Tarts, Milk Duds and sticky floors.

Today, with all the dangers to children that we see in the news, it's hard to imagine a time when the only real rule was to be back home by the time the street lights turned on.

We had a limited spiritual education as children. My mother would take us to church on Christmas and Easter—like most people. Because we had just moved to San Diego, and we didn't have any friends yet, Sunday School would be a great way to meet some other neighborhood children. We'd walk to a nearby church, probably to enjoy wearing our pretty homemade dresses of frilly taffeta and our white gloves. It was only when, one Sunday, I happened to pick a rose growing over the fence of a house along the way to church that everything went wrong.

He must have been deranged, because some old man came rushing out of the house, swearing and yelling at us. He swung a shining butcher knife over his head. We didn't stay to see if he was crazy enough to use it; but because of that terrifying experience, we stayed home on Sundays from then on, and that stunted my spiritual education. Occasionally, our folks would take us to a beach area church that was having Vacation Bible School so they could have a few hours on the sand without us.

Once we were all in school, my mom went to night school and took classes to complete her teaching credential. This allowed my mom and dad to share vacation times with the family. I also remember that they would use us as guinea pigs for all the different kinds of educational and intelligence tests their schools were experimenting with.

Please don't get the impression that I was a dainty china doll. Sure, we had music lessons (piano lessons, and I even played violin in the school orchestra), and we played dress-up; but Dad made us do yard work with push mowers, and my sisters and I rode bikes, played kickball, explored canyons and romped all over half a dozen beaches. Surfing wasn't on my horizon yet, but I can only imagine that many people viewed it as just another fad that would fade away. Playing with jacks would be all the rage when, suddenly, for no particular reason, hopscotch took over to be followed by marbles and then foursquare.

Our whole family was the outdoorsy type. Dad would load us all up with the tent in our station wagon (the minivan of the time), and we'd spend summer vacations camping along the Pacific coastline, all the way north into Oregon.

My dad was a hard-working guy, always having to be doing something. He worked a side job at a local hotel; and on top of that, he attended college for his master's degree. He'd decorate the yard with tiki torches and turned our front porch into a tropical garden. He also bought beat-up homes near the beach, and we would spend weekends helping to fix them up for resale. Then my sisters and I could take our canvas air-mattress rafts and play around in the ocean.

The beaches became our new playground as we fine-tuned our water skills on rubber rafts, riding waves all summer long. My parents soon found their favorite beach at La Jolla Cove. It was a snorkeling wonderland. We swam alongside my dad as we held our spears in readiness. I don't remember ever catching a fish by myself, because I couldn't bear the thought of killing one.

DESTINY

We learned to get abalone and let my dad get the lobsters. It was painful to watch them die as they were dropped into the boiling water when we returned home for dinner.

The Gidget scene (remember those beach movies?) was exploding in Los Angeles. Our cousins, who lived in West Covina, were very aware of this latest surfing craze. My mom's brother, who was an officer for the LAPD (Los Angeles Police Department), had four daughters. His oldest daughter, Kathy, was now sweet 16, and she decided that she wanted to try surfing. She figured that as soon as her family planned a visit to her water-immersed cousins down in San Diego, she would plan a surf venture.

My sister Debbie and I agreed to rent two boards and give surfing a try. My mom dropped us off at the Gordon and Smith Surf Shop in Mission Beach, a tiny hole in the wall, and we rented two boards for 50 cents each per hour. With the sidewalk baking our feet, we three girls took turns doubling up, carrying the heavy surfboards for a 20-minute walk up Mission Beach Drive to the designated surf zone. That left 20 minutes to surf before we had to walk back another 20 minutes to the surf shop, completing our one-hour rental.

Debbie and Kathy rode their first waves as I watched from the shore. Then, at last, it was my turn. I took hold of the board and pushed it out just inside the main middle breaking section of waves. I knew I didn't have much time left before we had to return, so I just went for it and took off on a little ankle snapper wave barely six inches high. When I reached the shore, I was told it was time to go back; so taking turns carrying the heavy boards, we walked back silently, inwardly focused on our thrilling adventure. I was so elated! Although I had only caught one tiny wave, I knew even then that this was all I ever wanted to do. All of my other goals in life disappeared: all of my plans

63

for the future—being a P.E. coach, my art, all of my other sports. All I could think of was surfing and how I could go out again.

Debbie and I pooled our savings and bought a yellow Gordon and Smith longboard for $30. Not too long after, we each had our own surfboard and were paddling out into the lineup at Law Street in Pacific Beach. We learned to surf by trial and error. Our first big error was trying to surf after covering our bodies with baby oil, which was the tanning rage of the day. It took us a few embarrassing days of constantly slipping off of our boards before the light went on! We became part of a small minority of avid surfer girls in a male-dominated world.

Debbie and I soon had surf knots on our knees and the tops of our feet. We rode 9-foot-6-inch, 30-pound long boards, or tankers, as they were nicknamed. They were heavy, which is probably the main reason most girls did not take up surfing. At first, we would both carry a surfboard to the water; but soon the guy surfers at Law Street would always insist on helping us out and even waxing them for us with the standard paraffin wax. Everyone always shared wax back then, as it was cheap!

We hung out with the same group of guys at the beach all summer long. Most of them were excellent surfers who only really cared about riding the waves. We always saw Skip Fry and enjoyed watching his amazing style. Not every girl could handle it. In the late sixties, surfboards were still big and heavy. Leashes hadn't even been invented yet; so if you wiped out, it meant a long swim in chilly water to get your board back. Wetsuits made specifically for surfing were in their infancy and were largely ineffective. While conditions were nothing like what Tom was experiencing back in New Jersey, a cold February morning in the kelp-filled Pacific could turn you blue and numb in a hurry. It made sense that most people considered surfing to be a sport only for tough, hardy males. Someone forgot to tell my sister and me. Even if they had, we would have paddled back out for more.

We improved our surfing pretty fast, but Debbie was always the best. She could switch stance so naturally and had the most amazingly smooth style going for the biggest of the set waves! We had fun paddling out on our knees and would stand up when going over an unbroken wave. Otherwise, it was a workout to plow through the wave with a push up when trying to get out past the breaking surf.

We didn't have leashes back in the 1960s, so we had to keep our guard up and not get hit by a flying board after someone wiped out. I began to surf well by most standards for women, and I won several contests back then, but I always felt second because of my sister's incredible talent.

One day, my parents would not let us bring our surfboards to the beach because the surf was supposed to get really big. We were so upset when we got to the beach, because the surf was perfect, with nice shoulder-high waves just like we liked it.

Once in a while, our family would go to Ocean Beach, and we would surf by the jetties, but my parents preferred to go to La Jolla Cove. They would drop us off at Law Street to surf because it was on the way to their beach. An unusual coincidence was that two other girls, named Debbie and Shary Melville, the same ages as we were, surfed the same break! Later in life, I found out that Debbie Melville got married on the same day as Tom and I did. Not to mention that my co-author, Rick Bundschuh, surfed Law Street at the same time and was best friends with my boyfriend!

After my older sister got her driver's license, we could get to the beach on our own. We borrowed my mom's car and started surfing Sunset Cliffs regularly. We liked the reefs, as it was an easier paddle out through a channel, not having to punch through closed-out sets at the beach breaks.

We damaged Mom's car several times and busted out the oil pan going over the bumpy dirt road at the end of Sunset Cliffs. Then we wrecked her driver's car door when we pushed the car out of the garage with the car door open in order to not wake up our parents at 5:00 A.M. But I don't ever remember my mom getting mad at us!

Soon my sister got a boyfriend, and I was surfing by myself. Abandoned, I started hitchhiking with my surfboard to the beach. At 16, I got my driver's license, and my dad bought me a car, so I didn't have to hitchhike anymore. He probably saved my life!

After I got a car, I would surf Sunset Cliffs every day at Abs. I surfed it for a solid six years. On occasion, I would go north up to the Cardiff area and surf Pipes. In high school, I made friends who surfed, and we would all pitch in for gas to go surfing. My friend, Pam Falgren, from high school tennis, also surfed. And she always made everything extra fun.

Not only were my parents teachers, but they were also history buffs. It was popular in the sixties to put murals on your walls, so we had the Greek Parthenon painted on our living room walls and marble furniture that looked like it came from Greece. Our specialty home deco was a statue in the living room of Venus de Milo almost two feet tall. This is one of the most famous sculptures of ancient Greece. How many kids grow up with that in their living room? I now see it as God preparing my eyes for what the future would hold.

After the shark attack, we had a week of interviews at a friend's house up in Kalihiwai Ridge. As soon as I walked into the living room, I was confronted with the Venus de Milo statue again! It was too close to home. No one else noticed it until I pointed it out. But it reminded me that I had grown up with that statue.